The Little Things and Such

Reflection Questions By

Roger C. Edwards, Jr.

EDVARDSON CREATIVE

www.edvardsoncreative.com

The Little Things and Such

Motivational Poems You Know and Love Now With Reflection Questions

ISBN: 978-0-692-21036-9 (Paperback)

Copyright © 2021 Edvardson Creative, LLC

For permision requests, please contact roger@thelittlethingsbook.com.

Disclaimer: With the exception of "Rainbows of Comfort", the motivational & inspirational poems and life quotes included in this book are not the original work of this Author and Publisher. Every effort was made to determine the original Author of poems labeled "Author unknown" or "Anonymous". Works with a named Author are either public domain eligible or were reproduced with written permission with acknowledgements on page 115.

Edvardson Creative, LLC

www.edvardsoncreative.com
www.thelittlethingsbook.com

For my Wednesday Night Groups

Thank you Stella for inviting me to coffee.
Thank you Elizabeth for inspiring me.

Keep coming back!
It works if you work it!

Author's Note

For more than two decades, I have collected hundreds of motivational poems and quotes. Whether discovered at conferences or seminars I attended, or whether the words were found posted in a company's break room or written on a coworkers cubicle, each inspirational message I read encouraged and motivated me. It's my desire that they do the same for YOU!

I would love to hear from you and know how *The Little Things and Such* motivated and inspired you to be, have, and do more.

Roger Edwards

roger@thelittlethingsbook.com

Table of Contents

Table of Contents

The Little Things and Such

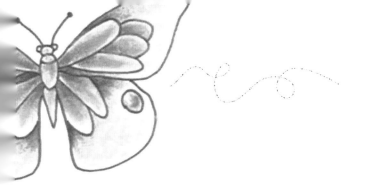

There's really no wrong way to use *The Little Things and Such* and its contents of motivational poems and reflections questions. Though, for individuals, friendships, couples, small groups, or classrooms, for example, we offer the following suggested use:

Begin this journey of self-discovery in a very relaxed state of mind. Set aside any thoughts of the past or the future and focus your attention only on the here and now. Make yourself comfortable and have a pen handy for writing down your thoughts and feelings while considering the reflection questions.

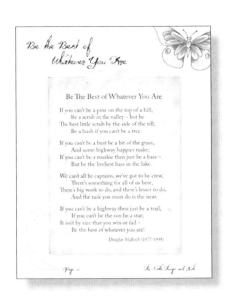

Step One:

Take a moment to read one of motivational poems or life quotes. In fact, we suggest that you read it multiple times. The poems and life quotes are in no particular order. As you're reading, try to internalize its meaning and allow yourself to get emotional involved in what the Author is conveying.

Step Two:

Then, turn your attention over to the reflection questions on the opposite page of the poem or life quote. Answer one question at a time in any order that you choose. Pay close attention to how you feel. If a question happens to elicit a negative response, stick with that question until you are able to find the good and write something positive.

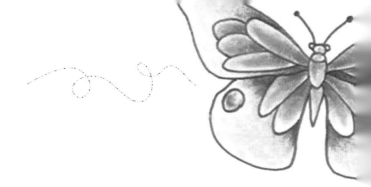

In the last few pages of *The Little Things and Such* we are giving you the opportunity to write your own poem or life quote and reflection questions. What inspirational message do you have to share with the world?

First, write down your poem or quote in the space provided. Then write down five reflection questions that will help readers extract the essence of your work.

Note: We have provided a printable PDF template that you can download from our website at www.thelittlethingsandsuch.com. Look for the free template link on the website's footer.

"And you? When will you begin that long journey into yourself?"

– Rumi

The Optimist Creed

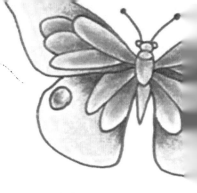

Promise Yourself...

To be so strong that nothing can disturb your peace of mind.

To talk health, happiness, and prosperity to every person you meet.

To make all your friends feel that there is something worthwhile in them.

To look at the sunny side of everything and make your optimism come true.

To think only of the best, to work only for the best and to expect only the best.

To be just as enthusiastic about the success of others as you are about your own.

To forget the mistakes of the past and press on to the greater achievements of the future.

To wear a cheerful expression at all times and give a smile to every living creature you meet.

To give so much time to improving yourself that you have no time to criticize others.

To be too large for worry, too noble for anger, too strong for fear, and too happy to permit the presence of trouble.

To think well of yourself and to proclaim this fact to the world, not in loud word, but in great deeds.

To live in the faith that the whole world is on your side, so long as you are true to the best that is in you.

~ Christian D. Larson

The Little Things and Such

Reflection Questions

1. Why is it so important to talk health, happiness, and prosperity to every person you meet? ....

....

....

....

2. Do you expect only the best? What do you expect? ....

....

....

....

3. Do you think well of yourself? What can you proclaim to the world? ....

....

....

....

4. Are you able to forget the mistakes of the past? Is this easy or difficult for you to do? ....

....

....

....

5. Do you agree that the world is on your side? Why or why not? ....

....

....

....

....

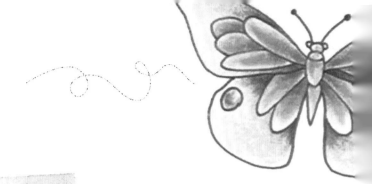

Thinking

If you think you are beaten, you are:
 If you think you dare not, you don't.
If you'd like to win but think you can't,
 It's almost a cinch you won't.

If you think you'll lose, you're lost,
 For out of the world we find
Success begins with a fellow's will –
 It's all in the state of mind.

If you think you're outclassed, you are;
 You've got to think high to rise;
You've got to be sure of yourself before
 You can ever win a prize.

Life's battles don't always go
 To the stronger or faster man;
But sooner or later the man who wins,
 Is the one who thinks he can.

                        – Walter D. Wintle

1. Do you agree that "success begins with a fellow's will"? What does this mean to you? ....
....
....
....
....

2. Give an example of something you want to do, but have not tried because you don't think you can? ....
....
....
....

3. What does it mean to be sure of one's self? ....
....
....
....

4. Is it possible for you to win even when you think you can't? ....
....
....
....

5. Write down an affirmation that you will say everyday that will cause you to think, "I can".
....
....
....

DON'T QUIT

When things go wrong, as they sometimes will,
When the road you're trudging seems all uphill,
When the funds are low, and the debts are high,
And you want to smile, but you have to sigh,
When care is pressing you down a bit,
Rest if you must, but don't you quit.

Life is strange with its twists and turns,
As everyone of us sometimes learns,
And many a failure turns about,
When he might have won had he stuck it out;
Don't give up though the pace seems slow,
You may succeed with another blow.

Success is failure turned inside out,
The silver tint of the clouds of doubt,
And you can never tell how close your,
It may be near when it seems so far;
So stick to the fight when your hardest hit,
It's when things seem worst
That you must not quit.

- Author Unknown

1. Have you ever quit? If so, how did this make you feel? ....
....
....
....

2. Do you agree that things seem to always workout when they seem at their worst? Why is this true? ....
....
....
....

3. How would you encourage someone to "stick it out" even though things may seem all uphill? ....
....
....
....

4. Describe how you might go about trying something again that you quit...
....
....
....

5. Why can't we always know how close we are to success? What happens when we are
not as close as we want? ....
....
....
....

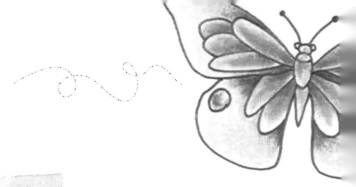

EXCELLENCE

EXCELLENCE is never an accident. It is achieved in an organization or institution only as a result of an unrelenting and vigorous insistence on the highest standards of performance. It requires an unswerving expectancy of quality.

EXCELLENCE is contagious. It infects and affects everyone in the organization. It charts the direction. It establishes the criteria for planning. It provides the zest and vitality to the organization. Once achieved, excellence has a talent for permeating every aspect of the life of the organization.

EXCELLENCE demands commitment and tenacious dedication from the leadership of the organization. Once it is accepted and expected, it must be nourished and continually reviewed and renewed. It is a never-ending process of learning and growing. It requires a spirit of motivation and boundless energy. It is always the result of a creatively conceived and precisely planned effort.

EXCELLENCE inspires; it electrifies. It potentializes every phase of the organization's life. It unleashes an impact which influences every program, every activity, every person. To instill it in an organization is difficult: to sustain it, even more so. It demands adaptability, imagination and vigor. But most of all, it requires from the leadership a constant state of self-discovery and discipline.

EXCELLENCE is an organization's lifeline. It is the most compelling answer to apathy and inertia. It energizes a stimulating and pulsating force. Once it becomes the expected standard of performance, it develops a fiercely driving and motivating philosophy of operation. Excellence is a state of mind put into action. It is a road-map to success. When a climate of excellence exists, all things come easier.

EXCELLENCE in an organization is important.

Because it is everything.

- Author Unknown

The Little Things and Such

1. Is it possible to be excellent at something? Why? ....

....

....

....

2. How would you know if an organization achieved excellence? ....

....

....

....

3. How is excellence "a state of mind put in action"? ....

....

....

....

4. Do you agree that when a climate of excellence exists, all things come easier? Why or why not? ....

....

....

....

5. In your own personal life, is excellence "everything"? Why or why not? ....

....

....

....

....

Be The Best of Whatever You Are

If you can't be a pine on the top of a hill,
　　Be a scrub in the valley – but be
The best little scrub by the side of the rill;
　　Be a bush if you can't be a tree.

If you can't be a bust be a bit of the grass,
　　And some highway happier make;
If you can't be a muskie then just be a bass –
　　But be the liveliest bass in the lake.

We can't all be captains, we've got to be crew,
　　There's something for all of us here,
There's big work to do, and there's lesser to do,
　　And the task you must do is the near.

If you can't be a highway then just be a trail,
　　If you can't be the sun be a star;
It isn't by size that you win or fail –
　　Be the best of whatever you are!

　　　　　　　　– Douglas Malloch (1877-1938)

1. What is meant by "we can't all be captains"? What is your preference, to be captain or crew? ....

....

....

....

2. Do you agree that the lesser work to be done is more urgent than the big work? If so, why? ....

....

....

....

3. If it isn't by size that you win or fail, then what do you think causes failure? ....

....

....

....

4. Do you feel like you are the best at what you are? ....

....

....

....

5. In what ways could you do the things you do in a better and more enthusiastic way? ....

....

....

....

....

Little Things

It's just the little homely things,
The unobtrusive, friendly things,
The "won't you let me help you" things,
That make our pathway light.

And, it's just the jolly, joking things,
The "never mind the trouble" things,
The "laugh with me, it's funny" things,
That make the world seem bright.

For all the countless famous things,
The wondrous, record-breaking things,
Those "never can be equaled" things,
That all the papers cite.

Aren't like the little human things,
The everyday encountered things,
The "just because I like you" things,
The makes us happy quite.

So here's to all the simple things,
The dear "all in a day's work" things,
The "smile and face your trouble" things,
Trust God to put them right.

The "done and then forgotten" things,
The "can't you see I love you" things,
The hearty "I am with you" things,
That make life worth the fight.

- Grace Haines

1. Do you think it's possible to do something small in a big way? ....
....
....

2. What are examples of little things you can do to brighten your day? ....
....
....

3 How could a small little thing have more of an impact on someone than a famous big thing? ....
....
....

4. Write down the names of five people you could do a simple thing for? Who are they? What little thing will you do for them? When are you going to do this? ....
....
....
....
....
....
....

Desiderata

Desiderata

Go placidly amid the noise and hassle, and remember what peace there may be in silence. As far as possible without surrender be on good terms will all persons. Speak your truth quietly and clearly; and listen to others, even the dull and ignorant; they too have their story. Avoid loud and aggressive persons, they are vexations to the spirit. If you compare yourself with others, you may become vain and bitter; for always there will be greater and lesser persons than yourself. Enjoy your achievements as well as your plans. Keep interested in your own career, however humble; it is a real possession in the changing fortunes of time. Exercise caution in your business affairs; for the world is full of trickery. But let this not blind you to what virtue there is; many persons strive for high ideals; and everywhere life is full of heroism. Be yourself. Especially, do not feign affection. Neither be cynical about love; for in the face of all aridity and disenchantment it is perennial as the grass. Take kindly the council of the years, gracefully surrendering the things of youth. Nurture strength of spirt to shield you in sudden misfortune. But do not distress yourself with imaginings. Many fears are born of fatigue and loneliness. Beyond a wholesome discipline, be gentle with yourself. You are a child of the universe, no less than the trees and the stars; you have a right to be here. And whether or not it is clear to you, no doubt the universe is unfolding as it should. Therefore be at peace with your soul. With all its sham, drudgery and broken dreams, it is still a beautiful work. Be cheerful. Strive to be happy.

-Max Ehrmann, 1927

Reflection Questions

1. Why is it important to be on good terms with all persons? ....

....

....

2. Do you agree that you are a child of the universe? What right do you have to be here?.....................

....

....

3. How can you become vain and bitter by comparing yourself to others? ....

....

....

4. How do you feel about love? Do you love yourself? Why or why not?...

....

....

5. What does it mean to "distress yourself with imaginings"? Why is this not a good idea? ..

....

....

....

....

RISK

To laugh is to risk appearing the fool,
To weep is to risk appearing sentimental.
To reach out to another is to risk involvement.
To expose feelings is to risk showing your true self.
To place your ideas and your dreams before the crowd is to
risk being called naive.
To love is to risk not being loved in return,
To live is to risk dying,
To hope is to risk despair,
To try is to risk failure.

But risks must be taken, because the greatest risk in life is to
    risk nothing.
The person who risks nothing, does nothing, has nothing, is
    nothing, and becomes nothing.
He may avoid suffering and sorrow, but he simply cannot
    learn, feel, change, grow or love.
Chained by his certitudes, he is a slave; he has forfeited his
    freedom.

Only the person who risks is truly free.

- Janet Rand

1. Why would exposing how you feel also expose your true self? ....
....
....

2. How does taking a risk cause you to learn, feel, change, grow and love? ....
....
....

3. Why must risks be taken? ....
....
....

4. Do you agree that only a person who risks...is free? What does this mean to you? ....
....
....

5. Have you ever shared your ideas and dreams with others? What happened? Is it a risk
that you would take again? ....
....
....
....

The True Joy in Life

This is the true joy in life,
    the being used for a purpose
recognized by yourself as a mighty one;
    the being a force of nature
instead of a feverish, little clod of ailments
    and grievances, complaining that the world
will not devote itself to making you happy.
I am of the opinion that my life belongs to
    the whole community, and as long as I live, it is
my privilege to do forth whatever I can.
I want to be thoroughly used up when I die,
    for the harder I work, the more I live.
I rejoice in life for its own sake.
Life is no "brief candle" to me.
    It is a sort of splendid torch
which I've got a hold of for the moment,
    and I want to make it burn as brightly
as I can before handing it on to the future
    generations.

- George Bernard Shaw (1856−1950)

Reflection Questions

1. What's so significant about being recognized by yourself versus being recognized by others? ....

2. Do you agree that your life belongs to the whole community? ....

3. Are you living your life like a "brief candle" or a "splendid torch"? How do you know? ....

4. What's your life's purpose? ....

5. What about your life is worth rejoicing? ....

Motivation & Management

People
Don't want to
Be managed
They want
To be lead.
Whoever heard
Of a world manager?
World Leader,
Yes!
Educational leader.
Political leader.
Religious leader.
Scout leader.
Community leader.
Labor leader.
Business leader.
They lead.
They don't manage.
The carrot
Always wins

Over the stick.

Ask the horse.
You can lead a
Horse to water
But you can't
Manage a horse to drink.
If you want to
Manage somebody,
Manage yourself.
Do that well
And you'll
Be ready to
Stop managing
And start leading!

- Author Unknown

1. What's the difference between a manager and a leader? ....
....
....

2. Do you think you are more of a manager or a leader? Why? ....
....
....

3. Are managers bad? What role do they play in the world? ....
....
....

4. How would managing yourself first, cause you to be a better leader? ....
....
....

5. Where did you learn your leadership and management skills? ....
....
....
....
....

The Power of You

Never give up on your dreams,
   Impossible as they seem.
When you feel your pursuit is through,
   Always believe in the power of you.
Even through the struggle and strife,
   Always believe in your gift of life.
Don't be afraid to express your view,
   And always believe in the power of you.

- Brenda McNeal

1. What's an example of a dream you gave up on? Why did you give up? ....

....

....

....

2. Is it easy for you to express your view? What are positive ways you could express your views better? ....

....

....

....

3. Do you believe in the power of you? What power do you posses? ....

....

....

....

4. What is your gift of life? ....

....

....

....

5. What do you do when you begin to feel that your pursuit is through? ....

....

....

....

....

THE BOTTOM LINE

FACE IT. Nobody owes you a living,
What you achieve or fail to achieve in your lifetime
    is directly related to what you do or fail to do.
No one chooses his parents or childhood,
    but you can choose your own direction.
Everyone has problems and obstacles to overcome,
    but that is relative to each individual.
NOTHING IS CARVED IN STONE.
    You can change anything in your life,
        if you want to badly enough.
Excuses are for losers:
    Those who take responsibility for their actions
        are the real winners in life.
    Winners meet life's challenges head on,
        knowing there are no guarantees,
            and give it all they've got.
And never think it's too late or too early to begin.
    Time plays no favorites and will pass
        whether you act or not.
TAKE CONTROL OF YOUR LIFE.
    Dare to dream and take risks.
Compete.
If you aren't willing to work for your goals,
    Don't expect others to.

BELIEVE IN YOURSELF.

- Author Unknown

Reflection Questions

1. Is there something in your life that you want to change? What is stopping you? ....
....
....
....

2. Why are those who take responsibility for their actions the real winners? Do you take responsibility for
your actions? ....
....
....
....

3. Who is responsible for your failures and achievements? ....
....
....
....

4. How are obstacles and problems relative to each individual? ....
....
....

5. Do you think its too late or to early to begin? Why or why not? ....
....
....
....

Take Time

Have you said to yourself or heard someone else say recently, "There just isn't enough time to do everything." The fact is, there never will be unless we make the time. An old prayer sums it up this way: "Take time to think, it's the source of power. Take time to play, it's the secret of perpetual youth. Take time to read, it's the foundation of wisdom. Take time to pray, it's the greatest power on earth. Take time to love and be loved. Take time to be friendly, it's the road to happiness. Take time to laugh, it's the music of the soul. Take time to give, it's too short a day to be selfish. Take time to work, it's the price of success. Take time for others, and you'll always be in good company and good spirits."

- Author Unknown

1. How is taking time to think, a source of power? ....

....

....

....

2. Do you agree that work is the price of the success? Why or why not? ....

....

....

....

3. Is it possible to manage time? Can time be managed? ....

....

....

....

4. What things are you not doing, that you want to do, because you feel there is not enough time? How could you make the time? ....

....

....

....

5. When was the last time you laughed? ....

....

....

....

SUCCESS

TO LAUGH OFTEN AND MUCH; TO WIN
THE RESPECT OF INTELLIGENT PEOPLE AND
AFFECTION OF CHILDREN; TO EARN THE
APPRECIATION OF HONEST CRITICS AND
ENDURE THE BETRAYAL OF FALSE FRIENDS;
TO APPRECIATE BEAUTY, TO FIND THE BEST IN
OTHERS; TO LEAVE THE WORLD A BIT BETTER,
WHETHER BY A HEALTHY CHILD, A GARDEN
PATCH OR A REDEEMED SOCIAL CONDITION; TO
KNOW EVEN ONE LIFE HAS BREATHED EASIER BE-
CAUSE YOU HAVE LIVED.

THIS IS TO HAVE SUCCEEDED.

- ADAPTED FROM BESSIE STANLEY'S 1904
ESSAY ON "WHAT IS SUCCESS"

Reflection Questions

1. What is your personal definition of success? ....

....

....

2. Why is it important to find the best in others? Is this easy or difficult for you? ....

....

....

3. What are you doing, or what have you done, to leave the world a bit better? ....

....

....

4. Is there someone in your life who has "breathed easier" because of you? ....

....

....

5. What is the value in earning the appreciation of an honest critic? ....

....

....

....

....

Time

Have you wished for wealth while dreaming of a goal
And thought that money was key to the plan?
Well, think again, for in any role
Time − not money − is the true currency of man.

Is it happiness you want, fulfillment of a dream,
Or will only power sate you, who fear to be an also-ran?
Well, reflect again on what success will mean.
It's time − not glory − that's true currency of man.

We are given one day to spend at each morn,
And what we do with this God-given gift
Will determine whether we are reborn
Or just waste away the sands that do sift.

So aim at the real treasure of man.
Think not about money or power or gain.
Rather, use the precious moments you can
And glory in time, ere it slip by and wane.

Robert B. Brown (1946−2006)

Reflection Questions

1. What is meant by "time is the true currency of man"? ....
....
....
....

2. Think of an hour glass... Now think of the sand above – nobody knows how much time we have left.
Now think of the sand below – we can do nothing about what's past. All we have is the here and now –
"the sands that do sift". Are you living in this moment – Do you "glory in time"? ....
....
....
....

3. What is the real treasure of man? ....
....
....
....

4. How do you spend your mornings? Are you grateful and thankful for life? ....
....
....

5. What do you believe is your God-given gift? What are you doing with it? ....
....
....
....

THE DIFFERENCE

I got up early one morning
And rushed right into the day;
I had so much to accomplish
That I didn't have time to pray.

Problems just tumbled about me,
And heavier came each task.
"Why doesn't God help?" I wondered.
He answered, "You didn't ask."

I wanted so see joy and beauty,
But the day toiled on, gray and bleak.
I wondered why God didn't show me.
He said, "But you didn't seek."

I tried to come in God's presence;
I used all my keys at the lock.
God gently and lovingly chided,
"My child, you didn't knock."

I woke up early this morning,
And paused before entering the day.
I have so much to accomplish
That I had to take time to pray.

- Grace L. Naessens, 1960

1. How does rushing into the day determine your effectiveness? ....
....
....
....

2. What can you do when problems compound and seem to get worse? ....
....
....
....

3. What prevents you from seeing the joy and beauty of each day? ....
....
....
....

4. What does prayer mean to you? ....
....
....
....

5. Write down a prayer that you could say each morning before you rushed into your day? .....
....
....
....
....

READ OUT LOUD DAILY

I realize that the power within me is greater for me than the power of another. That I have the power to control my thoughts and that my thoughts control my feelings and the way I see the world around me.

I realize that negative thoughts create negative experiences and positive thoughts create positive experiences, therefore I now decide to control my thoughts and think of the positive good side of me….and my world.

I realize that thoughts dominant in my mind will manifest themselves in reality. Therefore I now decide to keep before me a positive, happy picture of my success.

I realize the spoken word is the most powerful, therefore I speak good thoughts out loud and count my blessings daily, focusing my thought energy on the good of me, of you, of today and life. I start my day by getting myself up, I'm glad to be alive.

I love myself. I feel wanted, needed, important, and special. This is the greatest day of my life! I have joy and love in my heart! I am eager to **BE** *today! And give today that which I am. No one is exactly like me! I expect people to be glad to see me! The me I see, is the me* **I'll be!**

- Author Unknown

1. How do your thoughts control your feelings? ....
....
....
....

2. Do you agree that thoughts dominant in your mind will manifest themselves in reality? What does this
mean? ....
....
....
....

3. Are you in the habit of speaking good thoughts out loud? Why is this important? ....
....
....
....

4. Give three specific examples of how you can give today that which you are. ....
....
....
....

5. Describe what your positive and happy picture of success looks like. ....
....
....
....
....

Be Satisfied

BE SATISFIED...

Everyone longs to give him/herself to someone, to have a deep soul relationship with another and to be loved thoroughly and exclusively. But God often says, "No, not until you are satisfied, content, fulfilled with living - loved by me alone. No, not until you are giving yourself totally and unreservedly to me - to have an intensely personal and unique relationship with me alone."

"I love you, my child, and until you discover that only in me is your satisfaction - to be found, you will not be capable of the perfect human relationship I have planned for you. You won't be united with another until you are united with me, exclusive of any desires or longings."

"I want you to stop planning, stop wishing, and allow me to bring it to you. Keep watching me, expecting the greatest things. Keep learning and listening to the things I must tell you. You must wait."

"Don't be anxious, don't worry, don't look around at the things that I have given to others. Don't look at the things you think you want. Just keep looking at me, or else you will miss what I have to show you. Then, when you're ready, I'll surprise you with a love far greater than you would ever dream."

"You see, until you are ready, and until the one I have for you is ready, and until you are both satisfied exclusively with and the life I've prepared for you, you won't be able to experience the perfect love that exemplifies your relationship with me, and enjoy materially and concretely the everlasting beauty and perfection and love that I offer you myself."

"I love you utterly, I am God." Believe, and be satisfied.

- Author Unknown

The Little Things and Such

Reflection Questions

1. What first must happen before you're able to have a deep soul relationship with another? ....
....
....

2. Do you expect only the greatest things for your life? What do you expect? ....
....
....

3. What is the danger in looking around at the things given to others? ....
....
....

4. How will you know that you are ready for a love far greater than you could ever dream? ....
....
....

5. What's the difference between being content and being satisfied? ....
....
....
....

TWO SIDES OF A FENCE

When the other fellow takes a long time, he's slow; but when I take a long time, I'm thorough!

When the other fellow doesn't do it, he's lazy; but when I can't do it, I'm too busy!

When the other fellow does something without being told, he's overstepping his bounds; but when I do, that's initiative.

When the other fellow takes a stand, he's bull-headed; but when I'm doing it, I'm being firm!

When the other fellow overlooks a rule of etiquette, he's rude; but when I skip a few rules, I'm original!

When the other fellow pleases the boss, he's polishing the brass; but when I please the boss, that's cooperation!

When the other fellow gets ahead, he's getting the breaks; but when I manage to get ahead, it's the result of hard work!

- Author Unknown

1. Are you in the habit of seeing the good in others? Is it possible to be a positive influence on others if you can't see the good in them? ....

....

....

2. Can anything good come from bringing attention to the other side of the fence? ....

....

....

3. What recent situation or circumstance in your life can you relate this to? ....

....

....

4. Can you think of any life experience where there is really only one side of the fence? ....

....

....

5. Author Harper Lee wrote, "People generally see what they look for and hear what they listen for." Do you agree? Why or why not? ....

....

....

....

People Liked Him

People liked him, not because
He was rich or known to fame;
He had never won applause
As a star in any game.

His was not a brilliant style,
His was not a forceful way,
But he had a gentle smile
And a kindly word to say.

Never arrogant or proud
On he went with manner mild;
Never quarrelsome or loud,
Just as simple as a child.

Honest, patient, brave and true;
Thus he lived from day to day,
Doing what he found to do
In a cheerful sort of way.

Wasn't one to boast of gold
Or belittle it with sneers,
Didn't change from hot to cold,
Kept his friends throughout the
years.

Sort of man you like to meet
Any time or any place
There was always something sweet
And refreshing in his face.

Sort of a man you'd like to be:
Balanced well and truly square;
Patient in adversity,
Generous when his skies were fair.

Never lied to friend or foe,
Never rash in word or deed,
Quick to come and slow to go
In a neighbors time of need.

Never rose to wealth or fame,
Simply lived, and simply died,
But the passing of his name
Left a sorrow, far and wide.

Not for glory he'd attained,
Nor for what he had of pelf,
Were the friends he had gained,
But for what he was himself.

- Edgar A. Guest (1881-1959)

1. Which attribute of this, liked man, stood out the most to you? Why? ....

....

....

....

2. Do you know anyone like this man described? Who is it? And if they're still alive, have you told them

how much they are liked? ....

....

....

....

3. Is this the sort of man you'd like to be? Why or why not? ....

....

....

....

4. Do people like you? How do you know? ....

....

....

....

5. Has anyone ever said to you, "just be yourself"? What did they mean by this? ....

....

....

....

ALL IT TAKES

Size, I.Q., and looks don't matter..DO YOUR BEST TODAY
The past doesn't count..DO YOUR BEST TODAY
You can start where you are.. DO YOUR BEST TODAY
Knowledge is the only shortcut..DO YOUR BEST TODAY
We will learn as we go..DO YOUR BEST TODAY
All success starts small..DO YOUR BEST TODAY
Others will help you..DO YOUR BEST TODAY
Your best will get better..DO YOUR BEST TODAY
Your dreams start coming true..when you just
DO YOUR BEST TODAY

- Author Unknown

Reflection Questions

1. Do you agree that you can start right where you are? ....
....
....
....

2. Why does the past not count? ....
....
....
....

3. Do you think its true that all success starts small? If so, why do you think all success starts small? ....
....
....
....

4. Do you do your best each day? How do you know if you do? ....
....
....
....

5. Is learning as you go a good strategy to follow? Why or why not? ....
....
....
....
....

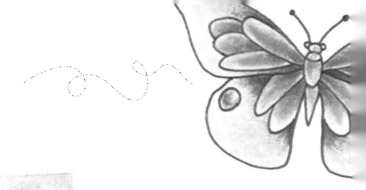

Winners

WINNERS take chances!
    Like everyone else, they fear failing
    And they refuse to let fear control them.

WINNERS don't give up.
    When life gets rough, they hang in
    Until the going gets better.

WINNERS are flexible.
    They realize there is more than one way
    And are willing to try others.

WINNERS know they are not perfect.
    They respect their weakness
    While making the most of their strengths.

WINNERS fall, but they don't stay down.
    They stubbornly refuse to let a fall
    Keep them from climbing.

WINNERS don't blame
    Fate for their failures
    Nor luck for their success.

WINNERS accept responsibility for their lives.

WINNERS are positive thinkers
    Who see good in all things.
    From the ordinary, they make the extraordinary.

WINNERS believe in the path
    They have chosen even when it's hard,
    Even when others can't see where they are going.

WINNERS are patient.
    They know a goal is only as worthy as the effort
    That's required to achieve it.

WINNERS are people like you.
    They make this world a better place to be.

                - Nancye V. Sims

Reflection Questions

1. In your own words, define what a Winner is. ....

....

....

....

2. Give an example of how "from the ordinary, you made the extraordinary" ....

....

....

....

3. What is the difference between giving into your weakness and respecting your weakness? ......

....

....

....

4. Make a list of as many of your strengths as you can think of? ....

....

....

....

5. Why is it so difficult to stick with a path without the support of others? ....

....

....

....

....

You Do Have a Choice

Be happy my friend
For you do have a choice,
You can sit and complain
Or stand and rejoice.
You can waste your life
With judgment and blame,
Or learn to forgive
And understand we're the same.

For all of us feel fear
And everyone knows pain,
Products of experience,
No one's to blame.
So let go of your past,
Your hurts and your fears,
Cherish each moment
And love life while you're still here.

- Author Unknown

1. Do you agree that you do have a choice? ....

....

....

2. Is it easy or difficult for you to forgive? Why do you think it's important to forgive? ....

....

....

3. Is there something in your past that you haven't let go of? What's keeping you from letting go? What

good would come out of letting go? ....

....

....

4. What do you do the most often... "sit and complain" or "stand and rejoice"? ....

....

....

5. Do you think it's healthy or unhealthy to feel fear? Why? ....

....

....

....

Walt Disney

Think of your values and principles

Believe in yourself and others

Dream about the future and things you
would like to see happen

Dare to make your dreams come true

- Walt Disney

The Little Things and Such

1. What do you value? What are your core principles in life? ....
....
....
....

2. What do you dream about? What would you like to see happen in your life? ....
....
....
....

3. What is one thing you can do today to begin working towards your dream? ....
....
....
....

4. Who in your life do you "believe in" and how did it come about that you believed in him or her? ....
....
....
....

5. What do you want to see happen in your immediate future? Why? ....
....
....
....
....

How to Be Enthusiastic Every Day

Believe in a higher being.
One of the greatest personal powers you may ever have in your life is a workable belief in a personal God. As surely as we need water when we are thirsty or food when we are hungry, we need a real faith in a personal God.

Make up your mind.
You must start being the person you want to be now.

Don't hold back.
Don't save enthusiasm for special occasions. Every day is a special day when you are enthusiastic. Bounce out of bed every morning with the throttle wide open. Then about 2:30 p.m. each day, open both throttles.

Hear your own voice.
Say "Good Morning" while at the same time thinking "I'm glad that I'm alive." Your voice will then say, "I like you." This doubles the power of casual "Good Morning."

Associate with enthusiastic people.
If you are standing in a mud hole you are liable to get mud on you. Don't let some pessimistic idiot control your thinking and rob you of your good.

Make definite plans.
Set your sails for your port of success. Do not drift with the tide. You are the captain and the master of every circumstance in your life.

Add variety to your life.
Don't get into humdrum living, be active, have hobbies, participate in sports, have fun.

Think you are some one.
Because you are. Did you know that without you, your God cannot run this universe exactly as He wants to? If you are important to your God, you must be someone.

Buy and wear good clothes
Look the part you are worthy of. Remember 95% of what other people see of you is bought in a store.

Make people like you.
Only one way, by liking people. Others are essential to us. We must make them like us.

Do one thing at a time.
Our minds respond to order and completeness. Don't get on your mental horse and try to ride in five directions at once.

- Author Unknown

1. How is having real faith in a personal God one of the greatest personal powers you will ever have? ....

....

....

....

2. Do you associate only with enthusiastic people? What effect does or would this have on your life? ....

....

....

....

3. What is the difference between confidence and arrogance? Which are you? ....

....

....

....

4. Do you make definite plans or do you "drift with the tide"? ....

....

....

....

5. In what ways are you adding variety to your life? ....

....

....

....

....

Brain Waves
For Leaders

"You are today where your thoughts have brought you. You will be tomorrow where your thoughts take you." – James Allen

"Leaders are not smarter than followers, they just think differently."

Everything begins with a thought: Victory begins with a thought – Defeat begins with a thought. What are you thinking? How are you thinking?

"Where success is concerned, people are not measured in inches, or pounds, or college degrees, or family background; they are measured by the size of their thinking. How big we think determines the size of our accomplishments." – David Schwartz

Leaders…...
DARE to dream
PREPARE the dream
WEAR the dream
REPAIR the dream
SHARE the dream

1. Why do leaders think differently? How are leader's thoughts different from thoughts of followers? ....
....
....
....

2. What are thoughts? Where do our thoughts come from? ....
....
....
....

3. Do you agree that you are measured by the size of your thinking? ....
....
....
....

4. Are you more of a leader or a follower? How do you know? ....
....
....
....

5. Where are your thoughts taking you? ....
....
....
....
....

Ladder Of Achievement

100%   I Did

90%   I Will

80%   I Can

70%   I Think I Can

60%   I Might

50%   I Think I Might

40%   What Is It

30%   I Wish I Could

20%   I Don't Know How

10%   I Can't

0%   I Won't

- Author Unknown

The Little Things and Such

1. Which do you find yourself saying more often – "I can't" or "I did"? ....

....

....

....

2. Is it OK that you may not know how to do something? Why is it OK? ....

....

....

....

3. Where do you think the majority of people fall on the ladder of achievement? ....

....

....

....

4. What needs to happen for you to progress up the ladder of achievement? ....

....

....

....

5. What's an example of something you thought you couldn't do but you did! ....

....

....

....

....

A Letter from a Friend

A letter From a Friend

I just had to write to tell you how much I love you and care for you. Yesterday, I saw you walking and laughing with your friends; I hoped that soon you'd want Me to walk along with you, too. So, I painted you a sunset to close your day and whispered a cool breeze to refresh you. I waited - - you never called - - I just kept on loving you.

As I watched you fall asleep last night, I wanted so much to touch you. I spilled moonlight onto your face - - trickling down your cheeks as so many tears have. You didn't even think of Me; I wanted so much to comfort you.

The next day I exploded a brilliant sunrise into glorious morning for you. But you wok up late and rushed off to work - - you didn't even notice. My sky became cloudy and my tears were the rain.

I love you. Oh, if you'd only listen, I really love you. I try to say it in the quiet of the green meadow and in the blue sky. The wind whispers My love throughout the treetops and spills it into the vibrant colors of all the flowers. I shout it to you in the thunder of the great waterfalls and compose love songs for birds to sing for you. I warm you with the clothing of My sunshine and perfume the air with nature's sweet scent. My love for you is deeper that any ocean and greater that any need in your heart. If you'd only realize how much I care.

My Dad sends His love. I want you to meet Him - - He cares, too. Fathers are just that way. So, please call on Me soon. No matter how long it takes. I'll wait - - because I love you.

Your Friend,
JESUS

- Author Unknown

The Little Things and Such

1. Are you the type of person who takes things for granted, or do you find beauty in all things and express appreciation? ....

....

....

2. Pierre Teilhard de Chardin said, "We are not human beings having a spiritual experience, we are spiritual beings having a human experience". Do you agree or disagree? Why? ....

....

....

....

3. Describe what it feels like to be truly loved by another human being..

....

....

....

4. What does unconditional love mean to you? ....

....

....

....

5. Do your close friends and family realize how much they are loved by you? How do you know? ....

....

....

What Love Can Do

While serving as First Lady, Pat Nixon was touring a hospital. She stopped by a bed to visit a young woman who had been blinded by rubella. After talking several minutes, she hugged the young girl and continued to talk affectionately and even sang to her. After she left the hospital she was informed that the young girl was deaf as well as blind. One of the supervisors stated, "I'm sorry, but she didn't understand a word you said."

Mrs. Nixon replied, "I knew that, but she can understand love."

                              - Author Unknown

1. Can love only be expressed in words? ....

....

....

....

2. Is it possible for our actions to not speak louder than our words? Why or why not? ....

....

....

....

3. When you give love, how do you know that it's been received? ....

....

....

....

4. Why is it true, that before you can give love you must first love yourself? ....

....

....

....

5. Are you capable of receiving love? How do you know? ....

....

....

....

....

How to Boost Your Mental Energy

1. Get out of your rut

2. Take more risks

3. Give yourself a "mental health" day

4. Believe in yourself

5. Visualize your goals

- Author Unknown

1. Describe a "rut" that you were in recently. How did you get out of it? ....
....
....
....

2. Are you a risk taker? How do you feel about taking risks? ....
....
....
....

3. Do you believe in yourself? Do others believe in you? ....
....
....
....

4. Why are "mental health days" important? ....
....
....
....

5. Describe a goal you are working towards. Can you visualize yourself achieving this goal? Why is visualizing the achievement of your goal so important? ....
....
....
....

Keep On Keepin' On

If the day looks kinder gloomy
  An' your chances kinder slim;
If the situation's puzzlin'
  An' the prospects awful grim,
An' perplexities keep pressin'
  Till all hope is nearly gone,
Jus' bristle up an' grit your teeth,
  An' keep on keepin' on.

Fumin' never wins a fight
  An' frettin' never pays;
There ain't no good in broodin' in
  These pessimistic ways -
Smile jus' kinder cheerfully
  When hope is nearly gone,
An' bristle up an' grit your teeth,
  An' keep on keepin' on.

There ain't no use in growlin'
  An' grumblin' all the time
When music's ringin' everywhere,
  An' everything's a rhyme-
Jus' keep on smilin' cheerfully,
  If hope is nearly gone,
An' bristle up an' grit your teeth,
  An' keep on keepin' on.

- Author Unknown

The Little Things and Such

1. What can you do when your "prosptect is awful grim"? ....
....
....
....

2. Do you agree that "frettin' never pays"? Why or why not? ....
....
....
....

3. When hope is nearly gone, what are your options? ....
....
....
....

4. What music is the Author refering to? What does this mean to you? ....
....
....
....

5. What happened the last time hope was nearly gone in your life? Did you
Keep on Keepin' on? ....
....
....
....

I Am Me

I AM ME.

IN ALL THE WORLD, THERE IS NO ONE ELSE EXACTLY LIKE ME EVERYTHINGTHATCOMESOUTOFMEISAUTHENTICALLYMINEBE-CAUSEIALONECHOOSEIT-IOWNEVERYTHINGABOUTME,MYBODY, MYFEELINGS,MYMOUTH,MYVOICE,ALLMYACTIONSWHETHER THEY BE TO OTHERS OR TO MYSELF - I OWN MY FANTASIES, MY DREAMS,MYHOPES,MYFEAR-IOWNALLMYTRIUMPHSANDSUC-CESSES,ALLMYFAILURESANDMISTAKES-BECAUSEIOWNALLOF ME,ICANBECOMEINTIMATELYACQUAINTEDWITHME-BYSODO-INGICANLOVEMEANDBEFRIENDLYWITHMEINALLMYPARTS-I KNOWTHEREAREASPECTSABOUTMYSELFTHATPUZZLEME,AND OTHERASPECTSTHATIDONOTKNOW-BUTASLONGASIAMFRIEND-LYANDLOVINGTOMYSELFICANCOURAGEOUSLYANDHOPEFULLY LOOKFORSOLUTIONSTOTHEPUZZLESANDFORWAYSTOFINDOUT MOREABOUTME-HOWEVERILOOKANDSOUND,WHATEVERISAY ANDDO,WHATEVERITHINKANDFEELATAGIVENMOMENTINTIME ISAUTHENTICALLYME-IFLATERSOMEPARTSOFHOWILOOKED, SOUNDED,THOUGHTANDFELTTURNOUTTOBEUNFITTING,ICAN DISCARDTHATWHICHISUNFITTINGANDKEEPTHEREST,ANDINVENT SOMETHINGNEWFORTHATWHICHIDISCARD-ICANSEE,HEAR,FEEL, THINK,SAY,ANDDO-IHAVETHETOOLSTOSURVIVE,TOBECLOSETO OTHERS,TOBEPRODUCTIVEANDTOMAKESENSEANDORDEROUTOF THEWORLDOFPEOPLEANDTHINGSOUTSIDEOFME-IOWNMEAND THEREFORE I CAN ENGINEER ME - I AM ME AND

I AM OK.

- Virginia Satir (1916-1988)

The Little Things and Such

1. It's true — there is no one else exactly like you! Take a moment and describe what makes you so unique. ......

....

....

....

2. What does it mean to "own" all of you? ....

....

....

....

3. Give an example of when you discarded something that was unfitting and invented something new. ....

....

....

....

4. How do we engineer ourselves? What does this mean? ....

....

....

....

5. What are examples of your survival tools? Where did these come from? ....

....

....

....

....

TRUTHS FOR YOUTHS

The late Phillip Gilliam, Juvenile Judge of Denver, gave the following advice to teenagers who asked, "What can we do, Where can we go?"

The answer is, Go home! Hang the storm windows, paint the woodwork, rake the leaves, mow the lawn, shovel the walk. Wash the car, learn to cook, scrub some floors. Repair the sink, build a boat, get a job, help your minister. Visit the sick, assist the poor, study your lessons. Then when you are through and not too tired, read a book. Your parents do not owe you entertainment. Your city or village does not owe you recreational facilities. The world does not owe you a living. You owe the world your time and energy and your talents so that no one will be at war or in poverty or sick or lonely again.

In plain words, grow up! Quit being a crybaby! Get out of your dream world and develop a backbone, not a wishbone. You're suppose to be mature enough to accept some of the responsibility your parents have carried for years. They have nursed, protected, helped, appealed, begged, excused, tolerated and denied themselves needed comforts so that you could have every benefit. This they have done gladly, for you are their dearest treasure. But now you have no right to expect them to bow to every whim and fancy just because selfish ego instead of common sense dominates your personality, your thinking, and your requests. Start acting like the maturity you seek - act like a man or a lady.

Most of all, in heaven's name, grow up! And go home!

- Phillip Gilliam

1. What's the difference between developing a "backbone", not a "wishbone"? ....
....
....

2. What's the significance of acting like the maturity you seek? ....
....
....

3. Do you agree that you owe the world your time, energy and talents? Why or why not? ....
....
....

4. What dominates your personality? Common sense or selfish ego? How do you know? ....
....
....

5. What, if anything, do other people owe you? Why? ....
....
....
....
....

Excellence Can Be Attained If You...

- Care more than others think is wise.

- Risk more than others think is safe.

- Dream more than others think is practical.

- Expect more than others think is possible.

- Author Unknown

1. When have you expected more than others thought was possible? ....
....
....
....

2. When was the last time you took a risk? How did it work out for you? ....
....
....
....

3. Have you ever been told that your just a dreamer? How did this make you feel? ....
....
....
....

4. Take a moment and write down the things that you truly care about Is it possible to care too much?
Why or why not? ....
....
....
....
....
....
....
....

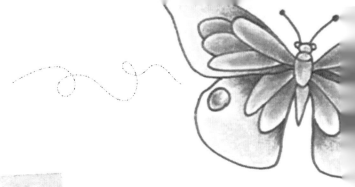

Courage

Courage is the price that Life exacts for granting peace,
The soul that knows it not, knows no release
From little things;
Knows not the livid loneliness of fear,
Nor mountain heights where bitter joy can hear
the sound of wings.

How can life grant us boon of living, compensate
For dull grey ugliness and pregnate hate
Unless we dare
The soul's dominion?
Each time we make a choice, we pay
With courage to behold the restless day,
And count it fair.

      - Amelia Earhart, 1927

1. Is courage required in order to get the most out of life? Why or why not? ....
....
....
....

2. Where does courage come from? ....
....
....
....

3. Are you a courageous person? How do you know? ....
....
....
....

4. Is courage contagious? Can you pass it on to others? Why or why not? ....
....
....
....

5. Why is courage the price you must pay when making a choice? ....
....
....
....
....

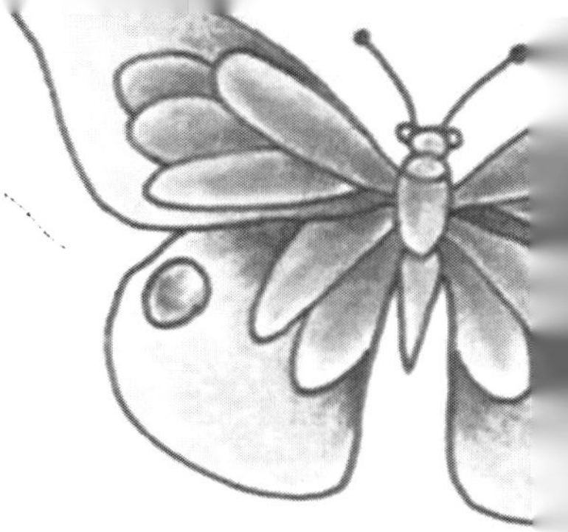

Geese in Flight

All of
us have
w a t c h e d
geese head-
ing south for
the winter fly-
ing in a "V" for-
mation. You might
be interested in know-
ing what science has dis-
covered about why they fly
that way. It has been learned
that as each bird flaps its wings
it creates an up-lift for the bird
following. By flying in a "V" for-
mation, the whole flock adds at least
71% greater flying range than if each
bird flew on its own. Whenever a goose
falls out of formation, it suddenly feels the
drag and resistance of trying to go it alone,
and quickly gets back into formation to take ad-
vantage of the lifting power of the bird immedi-
ately in front. When the lead goose gets tired, it
rotates back in the wing and another flies point. The
geese honk from behind so as to encourage those up in
front to keep up their speed (What kind of honker are you?)
Finally, when a goose gets sick, or it is wounded by gunshot
and falls out, two geese fall out of formation and follow it down
to help and defend and protect it. They stay with the goose until
it is either able to fly or until it is dead, and then they launch out on
their own or with another formation to catch up with their group, total
support to the finish!!!

- Author Unknown

Reflection Questions

1. When was the last time you helped, defended, or protected someone? ....
....
....
....

2. So.... What kind of "honker" are you? ....
....
....

3. What is your preference? Do you prefer to go at something alone or do you prefer to work with a team? Where did you learn this? ....
....
....

4. When you get tired do you allow someone else to take the lead? ....
....
....

5. Do your actions "uplift" others? How do you know? ....
....
....
....

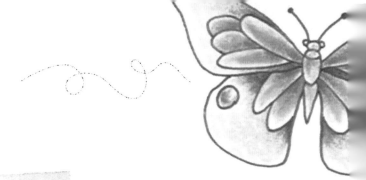

Listen

When I ask you to listen to me
    and you start giving advice
    you have not done what I asked.

When I ask you to listen to me
    and you begin to tell me why I shouldn't feel that way,
    you are trampling on my feelings.

When I ask you to listen to me
    and you feel you have to do something to solve my problem
    you have failed me, strange as that may seem.

Listen! All I asked, was that you listen,
    not talk or do - just hear me.

Advice is cheap: 10 cents will get you both Dear Abby and
    Billy Graham in the same newsletter.

And I can do for myself: I'm not helpless.
    Maybe discouraged and faltering, but not helpless.

When you do something for me that I can and need to do
    for myself, you contribute to my fear and weakness.

But, when you accept as a simple fact that I do feel what I feel,
    no matter how irrational, then I can quit trying to convince
    you and get about the business of understanding what's
    behind this irrational feeling.
    And when that's clear, the answers are obvious and I
    don't need advice.

Irrational feelings make sense when we understand what's
    behind them.

Perhaps that's why prayer works, sometimes, for some people
    because God is mute, and he doesn't give advice or
    try to fix things. "They" just listen and let you
    work it out yourself.

So, please listen and just hear me. And, if you want to
    talk, wait a minute for your turn: and I'll listen to you.

- Anonymous

The Little Things and Such

Reflection Questions

1. What are examples of irrational feelings? ....

....

....

....

2. How can doing something for someone contribute to their fear and weakness? ....

....

....

....

3. When was the last time someone really listened to you? How did this make you feel? ....

....

....

....

4. Are you a good listener? What makes you a good listener? ....

....

....

....

5. What's wrong with giving advice or trying to fix things? What can you do instead? ....

....

....

....

....

Important Words

Important Words

1. The six most important words
"I ADMIT I MADE A MISTAKE"
2. The five most important words
"YOU DID A GOOD JOB"
3. The four most important words:
"WHAT IS YOUR OPINION"
4. The three most important words:
"IF YOU PLEASE"
5. The two most important words:
"THANK YOU"
6. The one most important word:
"YOU"
7. The least most important word:
"I"

- Author Unknown

The Little Things and Such

1. What good can come out of admitting that you made a mistake? ....
....
....
....

2. When was the last time you told someone else that they were doing a good job? Make a commitment to
do this every day. ....
....
....

3. Do you value the opinions of others? When do their opinions matter? ....
....
....
....

4. How do you feel when someone says "thank you"? ....
....
....

5. Do you think putting others first is always a good idea? Why or why not? ....
....
....
....

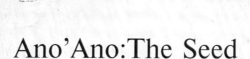

Ano'Ano:The Seed

And they were taught the laws of life...that their treatment of
others would return at last upon themselves.
Those who cheat will be cheated.
Those who slander will be slandered.
For every lie you tell...you will be lied to.
Brutality will meet with brutality.
We get what we give and to the same degree.
And not always from the same people with whom we've dealt.
But somewhere...sometime...someone will treat you in like manner.
The good that we do to others will return also.
For your kindness to strangers you will receive hospitality in far places
yourself.
Understand the troubles of others who come to you with their souls
bared...and when you cry yourself, you will be sympathetically
understood
We get what we give.
Like always attracts like.
This is the law and it is inevitable.
We cannot escape the results of our actions.
We get what we give..

- Kristin Zambucka

1. Why is it true that we get what we give? Is it fair? ....

....

....

....

2. How is it possible that you get what you give but not always from the same people with whom you

have dealt? ....

....

....

....

3. When was the last time you showed kindness to a stranger? How did this make you feel? ....

....

....

....

4. What sort of results do your actions bring? Are they good results or bad? What does this mean? ....

....

....

....

5. When was the last time you were sympathetically understood? ....

....

....

....

....

SERMONS WE SEE

I'd rather see a sermon than hear one - any day.
I'd rather one should walk with me, than merely show the way.
The eye's a better pupil and more willing than the ear;
Fine counsel is confusing but example is always clear.
The best of all the preachers are men who live their creeds.
For to see the good action is what everyone needs.
I can say I'll learn how to do it if you'll let me see it done;
I can watch your hand in action though your tongue too fast may run.
Although the lectures you deliver may be very wise and true,
I'd rather learn my lesson by observing what you do;
For I may misunderstand you and fine advice may give,
But it's not misunderstanding how you act and how you live.

- Edgar A. Guest

Reflection Questions

1. Why is the eye a better pupil and more willing than the ear? ....
....
....

2. When was the last time you saw "good action". What effect did this have on you? ....
....
....

3. Which takes more effort? Leading by "good" example or leading by "bad" example? Why? ....
....
....

4. What is one good action that can you do intentionally everyday? ....
....
....

5. Do you lead by example, by accident, or with purpose? ....
....
....
....
....

Keys For Living

KEYS FOR LIVING

1. ADD ENTHUSIASM TO WHATEVER YOU DO!

2. KEEP GROWING IN EVERY AREA OF YOUR LIFE!

3. GIVE YOURSELF TO OTHERS

4. LOVE MORE

5. MAKE MORE MISTAKES

6. LISTEN WITH MORE THAN YOUR EARS

7. CHANGE YOUR HABITS

8. BE A PEOPLE BUILDER

9. KNOW WHAT YOU WANT

10. TAKE MORE RISKS

11. KEEP DREAMING

12. ESTABLISH GOALS

13. FACE YOUR PROBLEMS

14. DON'T MAKE EXCUSES, MAKE GOOD!

15. DON'T DIE UNTIL YOU'RE DEAD

- Author Unknown

The Little Things and Such

1. What areas of your life could use more growth? ....
....
....
....

2. Where do habits come from? How are they changed? ....
....
....
....

3. List three problems you have been avoiding? What can you do today to face them? What do you think would happen if you did? ....
....
....
....

4. Why is it OK to make more mistakes? ....
....
....
....

5. Do you know what you want? Write it down..
....
....
....
....

> "Someday, after we have mastered the winds, the waves, the tides and gravity, we shall harness for God the energies of love. Then, for the second time in the history of the world, man will have discovered fire."

- Pierre Teilhard de Chardin

1. What do you think gives love its energy? ....
....
....
....

2. What holds you back from harnessing the energies of love? ....
....
....
....

3. What do you think would happen if you loved everyone you came in contact with? ....
....
....
....

4. Is it possible to love all things? Why or why not? ....
....
....
....

5. What first must happen before you are able to harness the energies of love? ....
....
....
....
....

My Comfort Zone

I used to have a comfort zone where I knew I couldn't
fail, the same four walls and busy work were really more
like jail. I longed so much to do the things I'd never done
before, but I stayed inside my comfort zone and paced the
same old floor.

I said it didn't matter that I wasn't doing much.
I said I didn't care for things like money, jewels and such.
I claimed to be so busy with the things inside the zone,
but deep inside I longed for something special of my own.

I couldn't let my life go by just watching others win.
I held my breath and stepped outside and let the change
begin. I took a step and with new strength I'd never felt
before, I kissed my comfort zone goodbye and closed and
locked the door.

If you're in a self-made comfort zone afraid to venture
out, remember that all winners were once with similar
doubt. A step or two and words of praise can make your
dreams come true. Greet your future with a smile. Suc-
cess is there for you!

- Author Unknown

Reflection Questions

1. What is an example of a time when you kissed your comfort zone goodbye? What happened? ....
....
....
....

2. Why are words of praise critical in making our dreams come true? ....
....
....
....

3. How is your comfort zone really more like jail? ....
....
....
....

4. Deep inside, do you long for something special of your own? What is it? ....
....
....
....

5. How do you feel when you see others win? ....
....
....
....
....

YOU ARE A WISE CREATIVE STRONGCLEVER DISCRIMINATING INTELLIGENTREFINED CHARMINGEXCITINGMAGNIFICENT PERSONABLEDELIGHTFULHUMANBEING

- Author Unknown

Reflection Questions

1. What new thing have you learned about yourself in the past twenty-four hours? ....

....

....

....

2. What is the difference between wisdom and intelligence? ....

....

....

....

3. What does it mean to be personable? Are you personable? How do you know? ....

....

....

....

4. What makes you .... you? ....

....

....

....

5. What creative idea did you come up with recently? Did you act on it? If not why not?

....

....

....

....

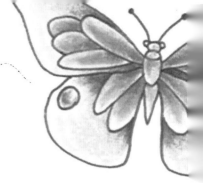

50 Ways to Say You're Doing Great

50 Ways to say You're Doing Great

1. You're on the right track!
2. Now you've figured it out!
3. That's the way!
4. You're really going to town!
5. Now you have it!
6. You did it that time!
7. Excellent work!
8. Good for you!
9. That's the best so far!
10. Keep it up!
11. Much better!
12. Good thinking!
13. Exactly right!
14. You make it look easy!
15. I knew you could do it!
16. Nothing can stop you now!
17. You've got it made!
18. Nicely done!
19. Nice going!
20. Superb!
21. That's the way to do it!
22. Keep up the good work!
23. Fantastic!
24. You're outdoing yourself!
25. WOW!
26. You're learning fast!
27. I'm really proud of you!
28. Marvelous!
29. You are really learning!
30. That's better than ever!
31. Well done mate!
32. Fine job!
33. You remembered!
34. Well look at you go!
35. Outstanding!
36. Congratulations!
37. That was first class work!
38. Right on!
39. I love it!
40. Sensational!
41. That's the best ever!
42. Right on the mark!
43. You're incredible!
44. I'm amazed!
45. You're getting better!
46. That's it!
47. I'm proud of you!
48. Brilliant work!
49. You've got it down pat!
50. That was first class!

- Author Unknown

The Little Things and Such

1. When was the last time someone told you that you were doing great? How did this make you feel?.........

....

....

2. How often do you tell yourself that you do a great job? Is it OK to do this? Why?...............................

....

....

3. Do you know anyone who is doing great? Make a commitment that you are going to tell them by the end of the day!...

....

....

4. Write down in your own words, as many ways to say "you're doing great" as you can think of.....................

....

....

....

....

....

....

....

If I Had It to Do All over Again

I Wouldn't Try To Be
<u>SO PERFECT</u>

If I had my life to live over again, I'd try to make more mistakes next time. I wouldn't try to be so perfect. We all have perfection fetishes. What difference does it make if you let people know you are imperfect? They can identify with you then. Nobody can identify with perfection.

I would relax more. I'd limber up. I'd be sillier than I've been on this trip. In fact, I know very few things I would take so seriously. I'd be crazier. I'd be less hygienic. I'd take more chances. I'd take more trips. I'd climb more mountains. I'd swim more rivers. I'd watch more sunsets. I'd go more places I've never seen. I'd eat more ice cream and fewer beans. I'd have more actual troubles and fewer imaginary ones.

You see, I was one of those people who lived sensibly and sanely hour after hour and day after day. Oh, I've had my moments and If I had it to do all over again, I'd have more of those moments. In fact, I'd try to have nothing but beautiful moments; moment by moment. In case you didn't know it, that's the stuff that life is made of - only moments. Don't miss the now. I've been one of those people who never went anywhere without a thermometer, a hot water bottle, a gargle, a raincoat and a parachute. If I had it to do all over again, I'd travel lighter next time.

If I had it to do all over again, I'd start barefoot earlier in the spring and stay that way later in the fall. I'd ride more merry-go-rounds, I'd watch more sunrises, and I'd play with more children. If I had it to do over again... but you see, I don't.

- Anonymous

The Little Things and Such

Reflection Questions

1. What are your perfection fetishes? ....
....
....
....

2. Do you agree that nobody can identify with perfection? Why? ....
....
....
....

3. Is it a bad thing to live sensibly and sanely? Why or why not? ....
....
....
....

4. Are you missing "the now"? How do you know? ....
....
....
....

5. If you had it to do all over again, what would you do differently? ....
....
....
....
....

RAINBOWS OF COMFORT

Sometimes when life gets gloomy,
and challenges and change seem like too much,
I often look to the sky and think a rather ugly thought:
"What if I were never born".

And as I curiously ponder this question,
I see above me, in the clouds,
the figures of all the people I have helped,
and the smiles I have carefully cut and pasted
on my friends faces.

These memories of joy and happiness
pass through me like a warm summer breeze.
And I once again, begin to feel,
that I have made a difference.
And even though it is true,
that the world can go on without me.
I am glad, and proud, that I am a part of it.

Focusing my thought energy
on the sky above,
I plea for a majestic voice
to tell me that I am special.
I long to feel needed and important.

The sky has never let me down.
It protects me from the joy-stealers of life.

And so it is for you.
We all look to the sky now and then for comfort.
And as you ask that ugly question,
as we all do in our own way,
and in our words,
I pray that you hear a voice
tell you how special you are.
You are special,
and you have made a difference!
And I pray to God
that the next time you look to the sky for comfort,
you see your rainbow.

- Roger Edwards

Reflection Questions

1. Have you ever felt like you wish you weren't born? ....

....

....

....

2. In time of need, where do you look to find your comfort? ....

....

....

....

3. Are you glad and proud to be a part of this world? Why? ....

....

....

....

4. What difference have you made? ....

....

....

....

5. When was the last time you saw your rainbow? What did it look like? ....

....

....

....

....

Ways to Approach Life

WAYS TO APPROACH LIFE

Self-Esteem
You understand that no one is more important than you are, and that no one is less important.

Courage
You see problems as challenges, and press on with a smile. You're able to take risks and deal with uncertainty.

Stress Management
You use your head instead of your back - you think things through and plan ahead to conserve your physical energy.

Creativity
You nurture your sense of humor. You use your imagination to come up with new possibilities.

Health
You give equal attention to health of body, mind and soul.

Motivation
You tap inner reserves so you're able to keep up your morale when everyone is losing theirs.

Communication
You are able to express your ideas and your needs clearly and concisely.

Quality Relationships
You relate well to people with different abilities and personalities. You are patient, kind, courteous and considerate.

- Author Unknown

The Little Things and Such

1. On a scale of 1-10 how would you rate your self-esteem? Where does your self-esteem come from? ....

....

....

2. When was the last time you used your imagination to come up with new possibilities? ....

....

....

3. How do you recharge your physical energy? Are your inner reserves at one-hundred percent? ....

....

....

4. When was the last time you expressed your needs clearly? What happened when you did? ....

....

....

5. Do you have quality relationships? What could you do to make them even better? ....

....

....

....

....

The Little Things and Such

Reflection Questions

1. ....
....
....
....

2. ....
....
....
....

3. ....
....
....
....

4. ....
....
....
....

5. ....
....
....
....
....

Thank You

The Optimist Creed (Page 14) - The Optimist Creed was authored in 1912 by Christian D. Larson, appearing in his book "Your Forces and How to Use Them". Christian D. Larson was an important New Thought leader in his own right and in influencing the founder of one of the major branches of New Thought, Religious Science, which also is known as Science of Mind. New Thought has influenced many, such as Norman Vincent Peale and numerous other inspirational, self-help writers.

Thinking (Page 16) - There are several versions of this poem including one called, "The Victor," attributed to a poet named C.W. Longenecker, and another version called, "Thinking: The Man Who Thinks He Can," attributed to a poet named Walter D. Wintle. The version given is the earliest recorded version and is taken from a publication of 1905 for the Unity Tract Society, Unity School of Christianity. Little is known about Walter D. Wintle except that he was a poet who lived in the late 19th and early 20th century. Nothing is known of the details of his life and indeed the name may in fact be a pseudonym. Although my research leads to Walter D. Wintle being more so the poet than C.W. Longenecker, I have decided to play it safe and publish the poem as "Anonymous."

Be the Best of Whatever You Are (Page 22) - Douglas Malloch (1877-1938) was an American poet, short story writer, and associate editor of American Lumberman, an adventure magazine connected with Edgar Rice Burroughs. His philosophy was one of "contentment" and being satisfied with one's lot in life. His wife, Helen Miller Malloch, was a newswoman who gained fame in her own right as founder of the National Association of Press Women.

Little Things (Page 24) - This poem is often attributed to an Author by the name of Grace Haines. However the two earliest known printed versions have no Author named. The version given comes from an advertisement printed in the Beaver Valley Times on December 5, 1959. No Author was named and for this reason I have published the poem as "Anonymous". And by the way, this poem was the inspiration for The Little things and Such.

Desiderata (Page 26) - Throughout his career, Max Ehrmann wrote more than 20 books and pamphlets and many essays and poems that were published separately in newspapers and magazines. His most acclaimed work was "Desiderata", originally published in 1927. Max Ehrmann died in 1945, well before "Desiderata" gained its popularity.

Acknowledgements

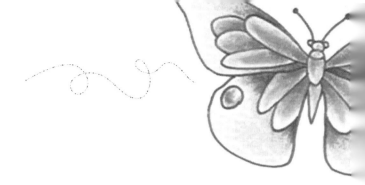

A Splendid Torch (Page 30) - The Anglo-Irish playwright George Bernard Shaw (1856-1950), winner of the Nobel Prize for Literature in 1925, acquired a reputation as the greatest dramatist in the English language during the first half of the 20th Century for the plays he had written at the height of his creativity. Shaw's complete works appeared in thirty-six volumes between 1930 and 1950, the year of his death.

Success (Page 40) - This popular quote about success if often attributed to Ralph Waldo Emerson, however it is most likely not by him. It has not been able to be found in Emerson's writing and it appears to be traceable to a 1905 publication by Bessie Stanley, although the wording is slightly different. This is most likely due to edits and adaptations over time. Her poem was written in 1904 for a contest held in Brown Book Magazine, by George Livingston Richards Co. of Boston, Massachusetts. Mrs. Stanley, of Lincoln, Kansas, submitted the words in the form of an essay, rather than as a poem. The competition was to answer the question "What is success?" in 100 words or less. Mrs. Stanley won the first prize of $250.

The Difference (Page 44) - Although this poem appears in many places and cards without any Author, it was in fact written by Grace Naessens in 1960. The poem is reprinted with permission from the Author:

"Many have asked me how I happened to write this poem. My second son, Chris took the poem to school for a poetry class. It wasn't long and it began to appear in published papers. So the poem became public domain and has no copyright. I have always felt much gratification knowing how much happiness and comfort the poem has brought to others.   happily give permission for the poem to be published and enjoyed, Grace L. Naessens"

People Liked Him (Page 52) - Edgar Albert Guest was a prolific English-born American poet who was popular in the first half of the 20th century and became known as the People's Poet. In 1891, Guest came with his family to the United States from England. From his first published work in the Detroit Free Press until his death in 1959, Guest penned some 11,000 poems which were syndicated in some 300 newspapers and collected in more than 20 books. Guest was made Poet Laureate of Michigan, the only poet to have been awarded the title. His popularity led to a weekly Detroit radio show which he hosted from 1931 until 1942, followed by a 1951 NBC television series, *A Guest in Your Home.*

Winners (Page 56) - Nancye V. Sims lives in the United States and is a resident of Lexington, Kentucky. She has written inspirational poetry for over twenty five years. Her writings have been published by Blue Mountain Arts in books, on cards, and other mediums, and can be read on hundreds of web sites. She is the author of "For Those Who Dream", a book of inspirational poetry. The poem is reprinted with permission from the Author:

"As the main purpose of my writings is to inspire and encourage others, I am always delighted to learn my humble words are achieving their God given purpose. I am more than happy to give you permission to include this poem in your book, and hope it will be a blessing to all who read it there, Nancye Sims."

Brain Waves for Leaders (Page 64) - James Allen was a British philosophical writer known for his inspirational books and poetry and as a pioneer of the self-help movement. His best known work, As a Man Thinketh, has been mass produced since its publication in 1902. Lily Allen, his wife, summarized her husband's literary mission in this way, "He never wrote theories, or for the sake of writing; but he wrote when he had a message, and it became a message only when he had lived it out in his own life, and knew that it was good. Thus he wrote facts, which he had proven by practice".

Brain Waves for Leaders (Page 64) - David Joseph Schwartz was an American motivational writer and coach. He became well known through his motivational publications and self-help books, especially for The Magic of Thinking Big, published in 1959. Schwartz, a professor at Georgia State University, also began his own work as a self-help coach and life strategist. Later, he founded his own consultancy firm focusing on leadership development called 'Creative Educational Services Inc'.

I Am Me (Page 76) - Virginia Satir was an American author and psychotherapist, known especially for her approach to family therapy and her work with Systemic Constellations. Satir often integrated meditations and poetic writing into both her public workshops and writings. One of her most well-known works, "I Am Me," was written by Satir in response to a question posed by an angry teenage girl.

Acknowledgements

Truths For Youths (Page 78) - Colorado Judge Philip Gilliam wrote this hard-hitting letter in a Denver newspaper in 1959 (called Open Letter to Teenager). Judge Gilliam was a tireless advocate for the young, wielding his substantial popularity to direct new resources towards preventing juvenile delinquency and helping those already in the system. Today Denver's Juvenile Hall, located at 28th and Downing Street, is named in his honor.

Courage (Page 82) - Amelia Mary Earhart was an American aviation pioneer and Author. Earhart was the first female pilot to fly solo across the Atlantic Ocean. She received the U.S. Distinguished Flying Cross for this record. As a social worker, she wrote this poem called "Courage," about making hard decisions; Eleanor Roosevelt kept a copy of it in her desk drawer. In 1937, her plane disappeared over the Pacific. The United States government spent $4 million looking for Earhart, which made it the most costly and intensive air and sea search in history at that time.

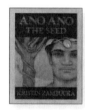

Ano'Ano:The Seed (Page 90) - Kristin Zambucka has won international acclaim for her inspirational, shamanistic books and definitive biographies of Royal Personages. New Zealand born, she has received The Queen's Service Medal from Queen Elizabeth II. The work is an exert from her book Ano'Ano:The Seed. This book has has become a classic in Hawaii and around the world. It tells of a group of seekers who are offered a "code of life": a way in which the suffering of mankind can be overcome. It's two sequels, The Mana Keepers and The Fire Lily are included in this volume. These collective works remind men and women of their oneness with nature and that they are "the Keepers of the Sacred Earth." Conflicting fires within us all are revealed, shadow-selves and ancient patterns are examined and understood, finally leading to the dawn of inner peace. The poem is reprinted with permission from the Author:

"Certainly, Roger...You may use the quote from my book Ano'Ano:The Seed starting with :'And they were taught the laws of life...' Thank you for getting in touch, Kristin Zambucka."

Sermons We See (Page 92) - Edgar Albert Guest was a prolific English-born American poet who was popular in the first half of the 20th century and became known as the People's Poet. In 1891, Guest came with his family to the United States from England. From his first published work in the Detroit Free Press until his death in 1959, Guest penned some 11,000 poems which were syndicated in some 300 newspapers and collected in more than 20 books. Guest was made Poet Laureate of Michigan, the only poet to have been awarded the title. His popularity led to a weekly Detroit radio show which he hosted from 1931 until 1942, followed by a 1951 NBC television series, *A Guest in Your Home*.

Someday (Page 96) - Pierre Teilhard de Chardin (1881-1955) was a French Jesuit theologian and scientist renowned for his pioneering field work in paleontology. His visionary writings on the reconciliation of faith and evolutionary theory aroused the suspicions of the Vatican and he was forbidden to publish on religious matters during his lifetime. After his death, the publication of his many books marked him as one of the most influential Catholic thinkers of this century - a mystic whose holistic vision speaks with growing relevance to contemporary spirituality. Often considered ahead of his time, Teilhard's writings have more relevance and impact on our current times than when he was first published.

Made in United States
North Haven, CT
08 May 2024

52282811R00065